A Secret We

New and Selected Poems

Ron Talney

Plain View Press
P.O. 42255
Austin, TX 78704

plainviewpress.net
sb@plainviewpress.net
512-441-2452

Copyright © 2010 Ron Talney. All rights reserved under International and Pan-American Copyright Conventions. No part of this book may be reproduced or distributed in any form or by any means, or stored in a data base or retrieval system, without written permission from the author. All rights, including electronic, are reserved by the author and publisher.

ISBN: 978-1-935514-55-8
Library of Congress Number: 2010928667

Cover art: *Stone Monolith*, Michael Selker photographer.
Cover design by Susan Bright.

for Linnette
as always

Carl B. Clapp
19749 Lasic Ct.
Oregon City, OR 97045-7942

Acknowledgements

Grateful acknowledgement is made to the following publications where a number of these poems, or earlier versions, first appeared: "The Broken World"; "The Broken Year"; "The Hunter". "Winter Poem", "The Man Who Wished For Death", in *The Portland Review*; "The Man Who Sat At His Desk" in *Cloudbank*; "Mt. St. Helens", in *Windfall*; "Tsawwassen Crossing", in *Lynx*; "The Dream", in *Encore: A Magazine of the Arts*; "Laugharne Castle, 2004", in *The Oregon State Bar Bulletin*; "The Dead of Night", in *Hubbub*; "Graves at Oysterville", "Social Graces", in *Fishtrap Anthology*, 2008; "Night Sky" and "The First Snow" in *The Oregonian*; "The Quietness that is our Name", "Everson in Fall and Disrepair", "How It Was", "St. Mary's Catholic Church", "Moving Quickly", "Reunion Speech for the Class of '54", "Malheur County", "Tracking", "Celilo Village", "Ecola", "The House at Lawton's View", "Where The Cowlitz Takes Us In", "Port Townsend", "The Lost Grandfather", "The Children of Masada" and "The Exchange" in *The Pacific Quarterly*;. "Lake Wilderness Tavern" and "Beers in Tangent" in *Fireweed*; "Cut-mango", "Elegy for my Father", "Ballet Dancer", Ars Poetica, "False Spring", "Gathering of Darkness", "A Night on the Mountain", "The Cabin in Winter", "Even Alone", "A Lifetime in Chilpancingo", " At Teotihaucan", "Poem for Alonzo", "The Names", "The Season of Pain", "The Angel of San Salvador", "The Poor of Mexico", "At the Shrine of Guadalupe" and "To The Deer Horns on our Cabin Wall" in *The Legal Studies Forum*, West Virginia University; "The Leaving" in *Northwest Magazine*; "The Sound of a Wooden Bell" in *Passager Magazine*; "Mountain Talk" in *10 Oregon Poets*, Prescott Street Press; "The Broken Year" in *Poets West*, Perivale Press; "Winter Poem," "The Dream" and "The Man Who Wished For Death" in *The Prescott Street Reader*, Prescott Street Press; "The First Snow" in *The Human Voice Quarterly*; and "The First Snow" in *If I Should Leave This Earth*, Black Ink Press.

The poems in Part I were previously published in book form as *The Anxious Ground*, Press-22 (1974). The poems in Part II were previously published as a chapbook, *The Quietness That Is Our Name*, Bohematash Press as part of the *Pacific House Series*, (1978). The poems in Part III were previously published as part of a chapbook, *The Broken World*, Stone City Press, as part of the *William Stafford Chapbook Series* from the Northwest Writing Institute, (2006). The poems in Part IV were first published as a chapbook, *Night Sky*, Stone City Press, (2009).

Contents: A Secret Weeping Of Stones

Foreward   9

One: *from The Anxious Ground* (1974)

Social Graces	13
The Gardener	15
Summer Grapes	16
The Dance Girl	17
Fears	18
Morning Poem	19
The Night Gazers	20
Going South	21
The Broken Year	22
Mountain Talk	23
Elegy For an Oregon Town	24
The Animals' Edge	25
Where We Grew	26
The First Snow	27
Turnings	28
In Memorium	29
Movements Into Fall	30
Reflections On World War II	31
Poem For a New Aaron	32
Names For Allison	33
A Taste Of Earth	34

Two: *from The Quietness That Is Our Name* (1978)

The Quietness That Is Our Name	37
Everson, In Fall and Disrepair	38
How It Was	39
St. Mary's Catholic Church	40
Moving Quickly	41

Reunion Speech For the Class Of '54	43
Malheur County	44
Tracking	45
Celilo Village	46
Ecola	48
The House At Lawton's View	49
Where the Cowlitz Takes Us In	50
Port Townsend	52
The Lost Grandfather	53
The Children Of Masada	55

Three: *from The Broken World* (2006)

The Broken World	59
Beers In Tangent	60
Lake Wilderness Tavern	61
The Hunter	62
How Could We Not Know	63
Winter Poem	64
If We Had Known Him	65
Mt. Saint Helens	66
Tsawwassen Crossing	67
The Exchange	68
The Dream	69
Laugharne Castle, 2004	70
The Dead Of Night	71
Graves At Oysterville	72
Coming Home	73

Four: *from Night Sky* (2009)

Night Sky	77
Letter To the Lost Daughter	78
The Arrival: PDX	79

After Her Death	80
Dream Poem	81
The Cabin In Winter	82
A Night On the Mountain	84
Even Alone	85
A Gathering Of Darkness	87

Five: *New Poems*

The Names	91
Poem For Alonzo	92
Cut-Mango	94
The Angel Of San Salvador	95
The Sound Of a Wooden Bell: Port au Prince, Haiti	96
The Season Of Pain	97
The Poor Of Mexico	98
At Teotihaucan	99
At the Shrine Of Guadalupe	100
A Lifetime In Chilpancingo	101
Ars Poetica	102
Parenting	104
Morning Poem	105
To the Deer Horns On Our Cabin Wall	106
False Spring	107
Ballet Dancer	108
Dream Cycle	109
That Other House	111
In the Stillness Of Names: A Family Portrait	112
The Hospital	116
The Leaving	117
Elegy For My Father	118

About the Author   119

Foreward

There are two kinds of poets: Those who convince you upon first reading that you, mere reader, could never make language do what the poet has it do, and those who convince us, by the magic of illusion, that we might step into the shoes of the poet and do ourselves what the poet has done. I have an affinity for the poets of the impossible and for poets like Ron Talney who by illusory assurance have us believing that his poems might, almost, be of our own doing. It's a theft from the poet, I agree, a theft I want to believe that Talney foretells with appreciation when he writes: "Friends, these words are yours, / are mine, are ours. / Take them, / and like a poem, become / the words we chose."

In *A Secret Weeping of Stones*, Talney has, without overreaching, and with no attempt to dazzle, created a collection of solidly convincing reflective poems that speak of neighbors and places, of towns and a loved daughter taken by death. We learn of death and what it has taken, and the poet who must speak of it and live with it. There is a "Letter to the Lost Daughter" and upon its arrival, we are then taken, poem by poem, into the depths of sadness, a sadness made bearable – almost bearable – as the poet charts a course through a "gathering of darkness" that forms around memory, loss and the dignity of survival. ("We fashion a future / out of air, / out of memory.") ("We have learned / the dance of grace.") In his eulogies, for the places he has known and a daughter, Talney speaks to a loss so profound that we beg to share its burden, knowing as we do that we cannot.

Talney's poems are "thick with memory" and leavened with sadness as he has us stand naked before necessity's shake-down. "Together we fondle / the knife of memory / until at last / it slips quietly / into your heart." The poet steps with us, or we with the poet, into a rich dreamscape of memory in which death sobers those it touches. Still, we hear no scream of fear, but look on with the poet, as "wolves lie / quiet in the snow."

Talney, like the gardener in the poem simply titled, "The Gardner," is "working through the crust so / darkly roots / take hold." What we have, in so many of these poems, is "taproots thrusting / deeper in the dark," an introduction to "the dark illusion of our lives / still defiant, stumbling, / searching for the light."

I find the poems in *A Secret Weeping of Stones* to be a blessing of grace. They are the work of a remarkable poet.

> James R. Elkins, J.D.,
> Professor,
> College of Law,
> West Virginia University,
> Editor, Legal Studies Forum

One:

from *The Anxious Ground* (1974)

> "A secret weeping of stones comes from each
> small crack my life has made in the earth."

Social Graces

Birds
across the lake
wheel and dip.

Fish dive
with endless
purposes in mind.

The light emerges
quiet,
as the earth

spins
weightless
in some memory

that gathers
ordinary
shapes of day.

A blank wall,
silent
but for shadows,

my future lurks
in all the local
mirrors. And somewhere

a cat
with feathers
in his mouth lies

watching
while my neighbor,
the lady-killer

continued…

tips his hat,
and smiles,
"Good Morning."

The Gardener

Worried by death
my neighbor
readjusts his yard each spring.

Even at night we hear
the click and rattle
of his hoe

working through the crust so
darkly roots
take hold. Not bright,

but strong, he bends
into the weight of earth, winter
melting from his face until

at last the blood turns
quick again, feeding
his dim mind

with dreams
and the final crack of tulip bulbs
discovering

a vacancy to fill.

Summer Grapes

Across the road
my neighbor sits,
propped on his sundeck,
eating cold-green-seedless
grapes.

The quick, selective hand,
the slow delight,
the obvious concern
for shapes
and methodology.

Trapped,
like something wild
in his teeth,
the morning shatters
bone.

And slowly
the heavy fruit
of all we loved
bends
into sacrifice.

The Dance Girl

The runway was
chin-high
to a straight shot.

Colored lights
fell across our laps.
Our grins were glowing

when she came on,
wearing 400 eyes
and a smile.

She winked,
and her eyelash
raked our faces

like a mortar shell.
She swayed,
and we became asthmatic.

She kicked,
and the place went
red as a wound.

We walked out
into the night,
her high heels

stuck in our hearts.

Fears

My barber hates me.
I feel guilty eating meat.

>   (night comes and I consume
>   the soft perfection moving
>   the slow air more
>   slowly. darkness
>   leaps in my eyes strange
>   as a handshake. a secret
>   weeping of stones comes from
>   each small crack my life has
>   made in the earth)

Somewhere a voice says:

>   "Next!"

My thoughts break toward
the funny light.

Morning Poem

This morning smoke
curves up
the hillside trees,

and last night drifts
across our faces
like a poem.

"Like smoke, we take
advantage of the wind,"
you said.

The Night Gazers

We lay about,
casual as stones,
waiting to see
the stars shine.

What a night!
What a quiet
hill! And, WOW!

What a
peace-loving look
we gave the universe.

Going South

Increasingly it is
more difficult to live
through January.

Its slow design of flesh
weights on the air,
an image losing,

like a pond, its edges
into white, defensive
snow.

Somehow the early flight
of birds said nothing
to this weather's turning;

but still its definitions poise
beneath our wings
going south.

The Broken Year

That year
we seemed to harden,
our hands
locked like lovers
or near-suicides.

March cracked
with bridges
washed away, and
backroads ending
where some town lay
crippled in the rain.

By June
the world spun out,
and weather rose
to furious heights,
taking our burned skin
to China, Mexico or Greece.

By October
you were dead,
a steering-wheel pushed
through your brain.
And now I walk your face down
highways lined with laughter,
find the way old
maps can die,
or simply lose their
grip on things.

That year I learned
the only language
I still use:
the sprung bone of your mouth

rising
from the concrete
like a kiss.

Mountain Talk

Up here night drops
like an eyelid.
And history is a heartbeat
spread out for miles.

Even a soft voice
rings these mountains for days.
And our words sound strange
just for having been spoken here.

Elegy For an Oregon Town

Somehow small towns go
hard. I used to dream you
into stone, a hardness flashing
like some violent river
in my head. And you would
rise like water churning white
to rest your weight
where human bodies
break into a thousand
arrowheads of bone, or
fishhooks riding
salmon to the shore.

But now you crack
like any tired face.
And I must reconstruct your
birth from lakes too deep for drowning,
from children dying
down your mountainsides.
You wrestle in my flesh with
real events, and reaching into
stone I harden with your weight:
a thousand arrowheads of bone,
and fishhooks riding salmon
in my throat.

The Animals' Edge

Surrounded by my fierce childhood
this town still lies,
secure and certain
as a dying field.

Its wooden walks
have found a mountain path;
and streetlamps burn the night
into a gray wolf thinking.

Here we lived so near the animals' edge
we could feel our lives divide,
tracking down some truth gone
puzzling through the dark.

Where We Grew

Where we grew
mountains were
part of the eye.

Rivers ran,
fresh and cold,
through darkened houses,

and animals would
come to stare
at our wild ideas.

Into the hush
of wagon tracks
we could lay our ears;

and arrowheads
found fingers searching
for their bloodstains

long flaked to dust
on lost trails
gone West.

Oh, Youth,
only such endless surfaces
could lead us to this.

The First Snow

The first snow and words
go to whiteness
quiet as a hill.

Into everything
that's us
cold settles deep.

Thinking beneath
the rawness of each gesture
we know this time
for what it wants.

From such experience
lives quicken to themselves:
questioning our lips with ice

we toughen.

Turnings

With all this weather's turning
I live
toward exposure.

I know how
the year progresses,
how it reaches away from time,

how it takes us.
I have watched
the children change,

their bodies growing
knowledgeable and shy.
They hold me

in the sun and laugh
to see their father,
human and afraid, stand stupid

where they placed him. Somewhere
I hear the martial music
start, the caissons rolling.

But I no longer move.
Guerrilla forces
gather in my eyes.

In Memorium

cold rain like
on a wall

a circus-tent affair
(there to protect
us we stood beneath
to honor

heads completely
bowed shocked
knuckles white as
sickness I

could see the lull of gestures
laughing out from
dark mahogany that grew so
many feet each

second you were
                            dying
      and
I recall how lilies seemed
in the oddest

       places.

Movements Into Fall

It is morning
and colder weather
is creeping up Boones Ferry Road.
A deeper wind is rising
and even our veins seem to wither.

The days move on,
brief as smoke
just drifting through.
The resolution to forget
is weighted as a stroke

that cracks its memory
across a goose-down pillow.
Last night a kitten died.
Five weeks of life whirled
into darkness. Slow-

ly a frozen hand
measures out the distances;
quietly an eyelash
trembles down. The movement
of a life breaks into pieces.

Reflections On World War II

for my father

You used to
dream in your socks,
your thoughts turning
red, like the moon.

They said you were "struck,"
that you didn't understand
the meaning of a dollar.

But still,
we waited for repairmen
(with the rest), drove
a funny car,

and you would tell us
things no man in wartime
really ought to say:

"Our neighbors down the street
have lost a son."

We give them sugar
even now.

Poem For a New Aaron

And Aaron shall be gathered to his people-
Book of Numbers

Create me Black,
for I am your new
father.

When all the sky
darkens into eyes,
and all the night

tightens its memory
about the moon,
I will be

the face that made you;
I will be your
new bone

however white.
And when you cry
for flesh you never knew,

and touch my
strange, familiar shape,
then all these

walls of skin
must break
across

the fiction
of our lives;
our dreams were right,

our faces...
only lies.

Names For Allison

i
Drawn from some deep
part of our fetal sea, your head,
wintering toward the light, cracks
the ancient bond of darkness, gripping
the bone of a new
freedom.

ii
What do we call you...

you who became so quickly
a household word, you
who burned on our tongues

like crazy?

iii
we call you:

word-flake; tree;
the petal of some flower yet
unnamed; a movement of wings; an arrowhead
chipped perfect; a fusion of remains; that dark
center of light captured at its once-daily moment of
breaking.

A Taste Of Earth

for Jennifer and Allison

It was my
second summer, and the
taste of earth was soft
as dreaming children
in their necessary sleep.

But now
it is my thirty-first,
and daughters
fill these rooms
as if they are the anxious ground
in which all
future shapes lie
waiting for some
final spark to flame
the substance of their wondering.

My darling seeds,
I watch the hardening take,
the tissue break
into its colored growth
and fill your (almost)
grown-up rooms
with taproots thrusting
deeper in the dark.

Caught by the energy
of your design, I
work parental fingers in the ground
and wait, my taste of earth, my
tender throats of
future sound.

Two:

from *The Quietness That Is Our Name* (1978)

"With noses to the ground we learn a river."

The Quietness That Is Our Name

Here
where each silence
rings the meaning
of our secret, deliberate

pace, a noiseless step
hardens
into rocks and trees
the poems we need.

Living this land
we grow, word by
word, into each

quietness that is our
name, into each
touch that is

our future need.

Everson, In Fall and Disrepair

For Doug

This town is 30 years of sadness
still. Here the names go bad. Light
breaks funny, and the Nooksack River
runs high water every Spring.

You find Kale's Cannery shut down,
the old church gray as death.
And north of where the school once
stood, dark houses harbor wind
off China and the sea.

Our neighbor, Mrs. Ham, lived
over there. Morning glories here.
Hortense died
the year we moved away.

You take the only road
your family took one day,
south, never coming back,
that woman smiling
while your sister cried.

And even now
you feel the town sink
heavy into dirt,
the dust of faces
blank beneath its stone,
the weight of clouds
and children calling: Years,

this is your home.

How It Was

    For Lyn

Sister, I wake
to your birthday
remembering

how it was,
that town still
living at the edge

of every dream,
faces we knew
leaning

from its streets just
right, and books
long out of print

that said
our lives
were really fun.

Today new towns say
what we've been,
years

gather in our minds
like photographs.
We live our losses

knowing at the back
of every town that town
we truly are still

throbs, slow and fading,
saying: Lyn, we slow,
but never die.

St. Mary's Catholic Church

Megler, Washington

Stern Mary by the sea,
the gray you are
is your religion now.
You bang your Bible
on the clouds, glare out
across the bay
at whales misguided
in their fun.

Years ago your arms
were Indian and gold,
your language odd off
sailing ships defeated
by those cliffs.
The river's mouth sings
danger to the gulls.

Hymns you chant mad
Indians forgot
a century before.
Chinook words fought
with Latin on their tongues.
Today their children drink
your sacrificial wine,
the old names ancient
in their eyes,
your spire still wailing "Jesus"

at the rocks.

Moving Quickly

i
Mother, we moved
quickly into
the thick of things:

you saying…
"remember the starving children",
some dog

howling his way
into the dark; the still
of winter on our lives; and you

my mother, saying…
remember.

ii
Night, stretching
like a vein of blood,
lengthens to the single
shadow of your face.

The hours creep
upon the whiteness
of these walls, and we
resort to magic,

dance about the
fire of your bed.
We follow as you
hold pain

deep within you
like a bud, your
sense of privacy still
strong as any

continued…

cracking of the mind.
You hate us,
even though we
cannot help,

and stare out from the
fragile fortress of your
rage. We were the only
crisis you had

lived for
since our birth.

Reunion Speech For the Class Of '54

My friends, no school should be this
bleak. Those rooms are still that
lonely gray, walls still shabby
in their disrepair, and windows
dark from years of hiding our defeat.

Tonight, those voices droning
dry as chalk, I think of locker rooms
and sweat; the cruel coach making men
from boys; of that sadistic nurse
who gave us physicals each Fall.

I see old Mrs. Peck, who liked me,
weeping her frustration at the jokes;
and Mr. Blake, who didn't, standing dazed,
his one suit ruined
when the ink bomb struck.

I think of fire-drills...
that black hole opening out to daylight,
swirling, and the teacher's sudden slap,
the long run home, and shame
the years can't ever take away.

Dear friends, we earned those years
like pain. What hurts is what we can't
let go. Even now I dream my ancient
need for girls in nylons moving
in their sweet, slow dance.

Our awkward arms embrace, our names
are shouting failure at the sky.

Malheur County

We break away from land
where breaking never ends.
All roads leave us
hot and dirt.

This bad-times County
earned its name;
Stinkingwater Pass is real,
and we deserve a medal
for the part we play.

Sun burns the Butte
to anger. In every town
kids harden into death.
Whatever happens

we become: tumbleweed, bad
wind, that carcass rotting
on the road.
300 miles west it stops…

But, oh Linnette,

that silence ringing
in our ears like stone.

Tracking

These mountains
toughen
to an ancient wind.

We need to
follow ice-cold rivers,
tracing history
like a frozen finger
through the snow.

Back to soap-rock, gray
flakes of shell,
and bone of fish gone
hard with accuracy.

With noses to the ground
we learn a river.
Recollection guides us

to its mouth.

Celilo Village

All along the river
towns are dead.
Celilo Village dies
but never dies.
The longhouse stands
half done and half
done in by weather
off the Gorge.

Kids play ball
against the sides
of trailer homes,
home but never
home, their eyes
reflect the gray
of local rain,
of wind, and that
despairing dirt that sings
deep down the bone.

East of Bingen,
towns like Wishram,
Maryhill, and Biggs,
a replica of Stonehenge
takes the hill,
some Druid outpost
where the only ritual
cries each night
for lack of silver
and that breath of legend
sacrificed to stone.

Old folks hold
our faces back

from pain, their hands
gone quiet
as that graveyard lost
beneath the river's
curve. Home
but never home,
we die but never
die. Silence here
is dialect for wrong,
and hardness now
the only word
for brother.

Ecola*

The ocean draws us
desperate to these rocks.
That man
who speaks our name says
love is here.
We are the seascape
moving in his eyes,
the bitter grays receding
like abandoned homes.

This place is where
our voids begin.
Where children
breathing water die,
and learn their way
among the bones of ships,
the cruelty of distance
on their fins.

Don't think
we ever love enough.
That man
who speaks our name
is really wind.
We walk this shore
of sad remains alone,
our silly bodies alien
in these tides,
Ecola booming
love me
to the sea.

*the Chinook word for whale

The House At Lawton's View

Devil's Lake, Oregon

This house is sinister
and cold. Tales of cruelty
or death drift
through its rooms,
believable but wrong.

Lawton's View:
some nobleman gone mad,
a hide-away for thieves,
a smuggler's cache too far
inland to be any good?
Surely there are bodies
in the cellar.

At midnight devils
name the lake in ways
the living never understand.
And Indian maidens
sacrificed at water's edge, still
sing this wind
for lovers gone to war.

Will water in the hand
communicate? Will vines of green
on green twist our dead mouths
to silence
and the final stone?

Moss-covered horns
above the door, porches
slumping into mist,
Lawton's View sinks
slowly to its knees.

Surrender,
and the world says: Yes.

Where the Cowlitz Takes Us In

for Owen

Remember
how each spring
the Cowlitz went insane?
How farms and houses
lost themselves to water,
horses drowned,
and crops became
the River's bed?

Remember
how that spring
we drove the Rainier route?
The bridges washed away?
That tavern
always closed to strangers?
Our fear of locals,
and their mystic need
for rain?

Remember
how at last
the water turned its rage to wind?
And how at Packwood
we crossed over safe,
the River's weight
dying off our tongues?

Friend,
it's spring again,
the River
still insane.
We lose ourselves
to weather
and the flood.

Home is where
the Cowlitz
takes us in.

Port Townsend

Here those towns we knew went
crazy with the ocean's
pull. In every house fish
rolled their bellies
to the air. Root cellars
were a hiding place
from Japanese balloons
that filled the woods
our sleep explored.

Each night
we dreamed again
those private streets,
that sawmill always burning
red on red, the school
where teachers practiced kindness
like a whip.

And now
in every town we are
all streets go
helpless to the sea,
their names alive
with fish and blood,
their asphalt begging
human from the roar.

The Lost Grandfather

Grandfather,
    after all these years I'm
    searching for you,
    searching through the cities
    where you lived:

    Winnipeg, Philadelphia,
    New York, Odessa,

    uncertain even
    of your name.

Grandfather,
    my lips now move
    along the walls that
    hold you. I tear them down
    stone by stone, looking
    for your eyes, your
    bones that are my bones, your
    face turning
    dark in my hands.

Grandfather,
    my old Rabbi,
    did you ever hold me?
    Did you take me
    into your ritual?
    Did you cut me
    with your holy knife?
    And did my small blood
    bloom on your tongue?

Grandfather,
    did you teach me those
    magic words that now
    somehow I know?

continued...

Today my father
takes his grandson
for a walk. I see them,
hand in hand, striding
toward the park, their voices
holding in the winter air.

Oh, my wandering Jew, my Ark, I
    watch them deepen
    with your touch,

Teacher, Man of God, I am your flesh.

    You are my bone.

The Children Of Masada

This is where the children died.
The Fortress of Masada stands
witness to their deaths.
Each father killed his own
and then drew lots until the perfect
silence was obtained. Roman soldiers
won the solitude but took no slaves.

They call me esoteric,
but these deaths go on and on.
Today a child still crawls these cliffs
and beats his life out
on the rocks below.
I paint his twisted face
into a grin, a photographic pose
my camera can't endure,
and watch bright flowers
bursting from his chest.

What place could live
by such a code of stones and dust?
Someday I'll dig in these remains
and find what children cry
when parents come with knives and hands
to love them from the rock.
No blood could really live this long,
and yet I hear the soldiers march,
their armor clanking closer
in the desert air. Father, Father...
love me with your spade, your club,
your esoteric hands,
and I will burst
into the only victory we are.

Three:

from The Broken World (2006)

"For we become whatever poems make real…"

The Broken World

> *"And so it was I entered*
> *The broken world to trace*
> *The visionary company of*
> *Love."*
>   *Hart Crane*

I see you
there
at the edge of land,

the deep, sad
arc of your face
dying

against the sea-
wall. In the distance
the buoy's distant moans
roll in,

minute by minute,
over the rocks.
And at your back,
weather

growing cruel.

Beers In Tangent

For Bill Sweet

Somewhere a tune begins:
That's all you get for
lovin' me. This town went
dead a dozen years ago.
But names like Wa-Chang
hammer out real faces from the air that
clang and swing like church bells
from the only place in town not
falling down.

With timber stripped and loggers gone
this place is left to
rusting rigs, to graves and
John's Café, where grade B stickers
line the walls, John's medals from some
undetermined war. He hates us
even though we aren't quite right,
and Tangent is the way it has to be
when rage congeals and everything we are

burns wrong.
We drink more beer, the jukebox
sings, and caught within its
pounding loss we sense a sudden
cracking of the mind. Then, fading
into song, we follow, like a map,
the pure act of its
dying.

Lake Wilderness Tavern

For Jim Fleming

The sun still rises
and our faces
reassemble to the dawn.
Doors of eyes reopen
and life goes back to
"Glory" and the weight of birds
hung over in the Wilderness
last night.

A huge bear sang his melody
from flowerbeds that mourned,
while lady skunks broke
tangible as glass,
and even Gable (Clark)
brought voice to bear
(God-damn it, Live!)
on pansies growing
final in the dark.

The matchbooks in our pockets
and the empty case of beer
say what we've been
when road-maps
turn to sound.
For we become
whatever poems make real.
And only words for human
work this ground.

The Hunter

I yearn
for the souls
of wild deer.
In every forest
I watch them
graze, and as they
graze I feel
their dark throats
slowly tighten, their
great, soft, velvet tongues
thicken in my mouth.
I am the sound
that brings them
death. In the deepest
of seasons
I bury myself
in their meat.

How Could We Not Know

How could we not know?

Here on the mountain
the river,
flowing past,
whispers the sea.

Trees
know their roots
however deep.

And birds
travel the world
but find that
single branch again.

Winter Poem

    On a line by Carolyn Kizer

Already it seems
like years have passed.
There
on the mountainside
I see your face turn
snow,
the eyes whiten,
and your mouth
fill with the slowness
of winter.

Here
in the valley,
lives go
gray with rain
and those countless
inconsistencies of flesh.

*We can cling to the dead
but the living
break away.*

I push my breath against the air
and watch its cold shape
disappear.

If We Had Known Him

For Lyn

If we had known him
we could not have loved him more.

Cradled in the stillness,
poised,

he would not recall
his emergence from your flesh,

the expectation of your pain,
the promises of death

that whispered through his muscles
as you labored.

He would not recall
the swept-out, dustless corners

where we waited for his sounds,
not knowing that the cycles of his life

trembled in the whiteness
of that cry.

Mt. Saint Helens

A mountain has us to the south.
Our way of thinking negotiates
across its frozen face.

It has guessed our bodies,
puzzled the dog,
and knows the kind of car we drive.

We should be staring at that mountain.
One needs to know this sort of thing
just to get along.

Tsawwassen Crossing

> *"The call of the unborn shapes*
> *leads us to the forms we seek."*
>   -sign on a wall in a hotel
>   in Vancouver, B.C.

Somehow the birds have
ceased to move
and hang
suspended in the air,

while waves move
black beyond the
movement of the boat.

Last night brought all
its own bad weather
crashing through the dark.

You held the shadow
of a fish between
your thighs, and

through the screech of
gulls we felt the
secret of an unborn face break
free.

The Exchange

For Mary

Slowly we move
into a new year.
"You know, it's funny
I should miss you,
you, who spent our time
like money."
I touch the coin
that is your poem,
bitter and exact.
We buy our losses
in the lines we share.
You know,
it's funny
I should miss you.
I, who spent words like time
or money.

Friend, these words are yours,
are mine, are ours.
Take them,
and like a poem, become

the words we choose.

The Dream

Your face floats in the dark.
The veins
are thick and blue.
I see the light
beneath the surfaces of bone
glowing like new milk.
And behind you
the black
ocean of night
rising and falling.

Laugharne Castle, 2004

For Jennifer

Here the voice is rich and green.
Dylan country everywhere.

Boats lie captured by the mud-flats,
waiting for the tide,
or conquerors from some far place
hidden in the mist.

We walk the esplanade,
the city walls,
see the fortress gray
against the ever-present sea.

And slowly we become
the dark of stone, the ruins' breath,
the moans and blood of all the years
that echo

from these cliffs.

The Dead Of Night

For the residents of Tanglewood

The order has gone out.
The houses
must be dark,
each bed
occupied and quiet.
It is time to sleep.

At night
the neighborhood
is everywhere,
its shadow
tracks our every move.
One by one
the windows blacken,
lawns lie still
and shrubs,
immaculate and sheared,
stand mute as body guards
outside our dreams.

In sleep
we roam from room to room,
floor to floor,
our odd, robotic step
the dark illusion of our lives,
still defiant, stumbling,

searching for the light.

Graves At Oysterville

These graves are old,
seem older even
than the sea
that daily still
defeats the town.
Across the Bay
renegades from South Bend
stole the courthouse.
The cemetery's all that's left
of water dying
in against the stone,
of empty houses
gray as wind,
as stone.
These graves are old,
but no one here
died old.
Alone and lost,
caught deep
where green breaks
solid into green,
they swam
the dark waves down.

"Lost at sea. Lost at sea."

Today, stone after stone,
we learn the names for water, salt,

bad weather.

Coming Home

I entered the world
through the voice
of my mother

calling me
home.

"Steady," she said,
and my hand went
quiet.

"Be true," she said,
and my eyes gazed
into the darkness,
steady as that hand she made,

clear,
as the way she was.

Four:

from *Night Sky* (2009)

"…*still your father, earthbound and small.*"

Night Sky

Child,
I look up
into the night sky
thinking
I might see you.

And light
from a dead star
a million miles away
touches
my face.

Letter To the Lost Daughter

> *"How shall the heart be*
> *reconciled to its feast of losses?"*
> Stanley Kunitz,
> The Layers

Daughter,

it could be yesterday.
April 8.
The year is always now.
However we live
hardens, sets its path,
shows us the way.

Even now
we see the crash,
your body broken,
lying by that freeway
in New Jersey.
Rain, then darkness,
did for you what we could not.

We hope
within that violence
there was peace,
a moment when you lifted up
and the pain
was gone.

Daughter,
in the midst of death
we still reach out,
we, the children
you will never have,

you, the parent of our grieving.

The Arrival: PDX

I heard the roar.
When I looked up
your plane, huge
and powerful, settled
into the airport lights.

"So far from there
to here," I thought,
"so far." And now
that moment is a blur,
a rush of time held

rich as your smile was,
waiting 'til I got there,
still your father,
earthbound and small.

After Her Death

After her death
there was only winter.

We held ourselves
beneath it, frozen,
unable to move.

After her death
no more death
was possible.

No spring came,
no summer, no fall.
Only the endless winter

locked in our chests
like stone.

Dream Poem

And so you dream of death,
and in your dream
you hold her loss
in your hands.
You turn it,
first one way
and then the other.

It is always the same.
Death never changes.

But then you waken,
the air
still with her leaving,
the room
still dying around you
terminal and strong.

The Cabin In Winter

1.
It could always be like this:
winter and the deep cold
invading our lives,
wind
and the swirls of snow
taking their toll.

We sit, you and I,
husband and wife,
father and mother,
before the fire,
before the altar
that is our past.

Where do we go?
How do we bind these wounds
that bind us,
prisoners of loss,
to a dead child?

2.
Now that winter is here
we walk out,
into the snow,
into the deep drifts
of silence,
up the road
through the forest
to the river.

That silence
hangs between us,
not silence really,
just the absence
of words.
It has been years.
The seasons click into place
their hard time.
We do only the simple things.

On this mountainside
we draw her breath,
like a third body,
into our lungs.
We fashion a future
out of air,

out of memory.

A Night On the Mountain

For Linnette

A night at the cabin.
We sit in the dark,
silent as trees,
and like trees
we sway gently.

I want to tell you
how much I miss her.
But you know me too well.
"She is everywhere we are,"
you say.

And as you speak
the night we are
deepens,
spreads itself
deeper and deeper
into the forest,

into the lives
of animals
and stones.

Even Alone

1.
Even alone
we are never alone.
She is the air
we breathe,

her form
a kind of darkness
that fills us
with her leaving.

At night
she rattles the door,
begs forgiveness,
holds us in her arms.

We dream of morning.

2.
It has been years.
We have learned
the dance of grace.

A small bird
comes to the feeder.
In the winter air
he sits alone,

searching.
We watch his progress,
know the uncertainty
by which he lives.

continued…

Soon it will be spring again,
an anniversary of sorts,
a rounding off of time.

We reach out.
The bird is gone.

3.
In this place,
this place of stones,
this place

where death lives,
where everyone
is young,

where time
holds us
like the children

we are,
we gather
to say again,

"We love you",
to hold again
the disappearing face,

to trace
the distance
by which we live,

the silence.

A Gathering Of Darkness

So tell us
that we loved her;
that we were held on her word's edge
as if by magic;
that somewhere mountains rise,
casting shadows like a weight,
splitting the earth
with her incredible silence,

and we will whisper "daughter, sister",
out upon this
gathering of darkness.

Five:

New Poems

*"And slowly, slowly
all these wounds we've shared reopen."*

The Names

Port Isabel Detention Center,
Rio Grande Valley, Texas

Under the Texas sun,
into the dust
you scratch your name,
the names of your wife,
your children,
your town
so far away.

El Salvador!
Another time,
so green, so lush,
those mountains, jungles
thick with memory
and fear.

Here
the prison yard is hot,
is crowded.
Men in orange jumpsuits
line the fences,
standing,
sitting.

The air is quiet.
No one moves.
Dust settles in.

The names
begin to disappear.

Poem For Alonzo

Port Isabel Detention Center,
Rio Grande Valley, Texas

"In El Salvador
it is easier to die
than live,"
you say.

I see death
etched in the way you
stare off
into the distance
we call Texas.

I trace the ruin in your face,
the collapse of bone,
your eyes,
tiny and sad.

How many sisters raped?
How many brothers dead?
How many bodies
by the road?

This far from San Vicente
your hands still move
against the steel,
against barbed wire

that even here
contains you.
"No recuerdo nada mas,"
you say.
"I remember nothing more."

I nod.
Together we fondle
the knife of memory
until at last

it slips quietly
into your heart,
the words now

pouring from your lips
like blood.

Cut-Mango

Father,
for the first time
since your death
I use your knife,
the tiny one
you always carried.

I am here,
in El Salvador,
here, in my hotel,
peeling a mango.

It is hot. Below
the streets are crowded.
Smells
from pupuserias
rise into the spaces
of the alleyway
outside my window.

I think of how
in better days
you might have been here too.

Carefully
I cut the fruit.
Carefully I clean
and fold the blade.

Here in El Salvador
at last
we are at peace.
And, Father,
here at last
cut-mango tastes

so sweet.

The Angel Of San Salvador

My name is Angel,
Angel Bonilla.
They call me
El angel de muerte,
The angel of death.

This is my job.
Each morning early
I drive my truck
through the city streets,
looking for the dead,
dead children, homeless,

huddled in doorways,
their tiny bodies
stiff with cold and hunger
they no longer feel.
I stack them, one by one,
onto the truck's bed,
the only bed they've ever known.

Outside the city
an open pit
contains what's left of youth.
I throw them in,
with bags of lye.
Then on each small corpse

I place a rose.

The Sound Of a Wooden Bell: Port au Prince, Haiti

"No one listens to the cries of the poor,
or the sound of a wooden bell."
Haitian Proverb

It is morning
on Delmas Avenue.

The street is crowded,
noisy.
Tap-taps rumble past.

Venders hawk their wares:
bananas, nuts and cigarettes.

A mother holds out her hand,
holds out her child, "America, she pleads,
"America."

I shake my head.
And somewhere

deep beneath her gaze
I hear
the sound of a wooden bell.

The Season Of Pain

> *"The season of pain is never over*
> *until the sky begins to cry."*
> Haitian proverb

Today
the sky began to cry.
But the season of pain
was not over.

Bombs fell on Lebanon,
rockets on Israel.
Shiites killed Sunnis,
Sunnis killed Shiites.

Hezbollah, Hamas,
a call for genocide.
Today the sky cried pain.
It is the season.

The Poor Of Mexico

There are no poor in Mexico.

Our guide, Raul, says
beggars in the city's streets
are really
rich folk from the country.

Out in the desert
our guide, Manuel, says
all those
broken, tired men we see
have really fancy
homes in Chilpancingo.

There are no poor in Mexico.
We know.
We've been there;
seen with our own eyes.

At Teotihaucan

From the pyramid
they could be ants
or soldiers.

Never children,
beggars, hawkers,
or Abuelito

guarding
Quetzacoatl's tomb.
Up here sun burns

the ancient temples
blue.
We climb and climb

until our
fat hearts
pound and swell.

We gasp, lie back,
await that final
touch of stone,

that cool obsidian.

At the Shrine Of Guadalupe

Slowly,
across the cobblestones,
toward incense
and the chanting priest
they crawl,

their hands
weaving the air
like dancers,
the hard-earned coins
floating from their lips

like prayers.

A Lifetime In Chilpancingo

It is morning
in Chilpancingo.

The lizard
who spent the night
clutching our wall
is gone.

He was no prisoner.

Outside, already,
peddlers are
working the streets,
boys, girls, little old men.

They sell nuts and puppets,
cigarettes and cherries.

I count the pesos
in my wallet.
Enough for a lifetime

if you make it quick.

Ars Poetica

Like all poems
this one
starts out short.

Gradually
it grows,
word by word.

Eventually
it fills the page,
reaching out

over the edge of the pad,
eating voraciously
tables, chairs,

lamps, my arm.
Nothing is safe
anymore.

Where will it end,
this poem?
Will there be

peace in our time?
I call for U.N. involvement,
disarmament talks.

Nothing works.
The poem moves on,
its path

wider and wider,
all life threatened,
the very atmosphere

at risk.
Uncle, I cry,
Uncle,

my white handkerchief
waving, my tongue
swollen

with surrender.

Parenting

No matter where we go,
no matter what we do,
the children
are everywhere.

We hide
behind doors, under beds,
in the basement.
It does no good.

Even in our dreams
they find us.
They suddenly appear,
grinning their

ever-loving, ever-lasting
shit-eating grins.
In the silent dark
they fondle our hearts

like dice.

Morning Poem

Each morning
you wake
to the ritual of lost causes,
the mystery of clothing,
another childhood
dead in its tracks.

Outside, the elm tree
takes on light.
A new day
settles in.
Slowly you assume
the dark of your face,

your only chance to survive
grinning
from ear to ear.

To the Deer Horns On Our Cabin Wall

I think
how fine your features
must have been,

the long snout,
the ears, the eyes,
your great, soft tongue

working the lichen.
It must have been a shock,
not knowing

what had happened,
knowing that you were,
suddenly, for no reason

dying.
Did you suffer?
Did you charge, madly,

into the brush?
Or did you
fall to your knees,

your delicate knees,
the blood rising
in your throat

like a scream,
the bullet
caught in your heart?

False Spring

What can we ever know
of spring that comes too soon,
too late,
or not at all?

What can we know
of time
that alters what our flesh
has been, or is, or will be?

What can we ever know
of love, that comes too late,
too soon,
or not at all?

Ballet Dancer

    for Maria Grande, (1937-1998)

Maria,
this poem is for you.
It's been years.
Today
I read the obituary,
cold facts:
breast cancer, a husband,
children, grandchildren,
an international career.

Even after all these years
the silent hallways of our lives
resound, echo
with our past.

For you
it was always the dance.
For me, the smile.
You once told me
dancers smile when the feet
go wrong,
a diversion for the eye.

So now I think of you,
your body lost
to its slow dance with pain,
your smile still
so right
even death
must have given you

    flowers, applause,
    a standing ovation.

Dream Cycle

> *"And they will dream of her*
> *who have not known her,*
> *and ache and ache*
> *for that lost limb forever."*
> Carolyn Kizer

In my dream
I walk
to your door.

I knock.
You are not
there.

But still
the door of your eye
swings open.

I enter.
At the back of your head
I throw myself

into a chair.
I sink deeply
into its cushions.

In the kitchen
I gaze fondly
at hard-boiled eggs.

In the bathroom,
your brush
tangled with dark hair.

continued…

In the bedrooms
I lie down.
Moonlight

fills my mouth.
I dream.
And in my dream

I walk to your door.
I knock.
You are not there.

But still,
the door of your eye
swings open.

That Other House

In that other house
you are
still a child.

Now you are six;
now you are
eleven.

Childhood moves
through you
like a dream, lays

over you
its long, dark
blanket.

Here,
in your mother's arms
you drift.

Deep,
beneath her
lullaby of flesh

you wait…
that child you have been,
that other house

you are.

In the Stillness Of Names:
A Family Portrait

○

It is 1905.
Odessa, Russia.
The courtyard
of our home.

The Cossack soldiers march,
they shout,
they sing.

The child is dead.
Her body
blooms with machine gun fire.

Her father
takes her
into his arms.

They disappear.

○

It is 1943.
La Grande, Oregon.
The New World.
We are together again.
My sister holds me.
She dresses me
in baby clothes.

She pushes me
down 8th Street
in the pram,
the only one in town.

On Adams Avenue
the soldiers march,
they shout,
they sing.

It is 1943.
There is no meat,
no sugar.

○

Through the trees
the flat, white
face of the moon
rises.

In the hills
above the town
wolves lie
quiet in the snow.

In front of Bonnenkamp's
the old men sit,
They watch the hills,
waiting for some sign.

○

It is 1960.
Another child
is dead.

The long snake
of his birth
is ended.

continued…

Deformed,
he takes on perfection
like air,

like stone.

○

It is 1988.
Beside a turnpike in New Jersey,
a child lies
broken in the rain.

In the midst of wreckage
she stares
from her cage
of bones and skin.

Her mouth
puckers with a new freedom.

○

It is 1905.
Odessa, Russia.
The courtyard
of our home.

Again,
the soldiers march,
they shout
they sing.

Our father
takes us
into his arms.

In the stillness of names
we lie down.

And slowly, slowly
all these wounds we've shared

reopen.

The Hospital

Somewhere,
in the quiet darkness
machinery
begins to hum.

A buzzer sounds.

Even now
they think you
merely sleep.

Your children
move about the bed,
their slow dance

beautiful as death.
Your breath
dissolves.

And in the paleness
of your skin
events begin to drift and drift…

like snow.

The Leaving

All night I watched
the dark failure of your skin,
the acting out of breath,
the dying light.

"Don't leave," I said,
and as I spoke you turned,
turned slowly,
like a great fish rolling
in the death-pond of your bed.

I touched your lips, your eyes,
the hollow remnants of your face;
bent down and finally kissed
your ash-bone cheek.

Elegy For My Father

Father,
I see you
moving back
into the age of shadows,
those years of shame
you clutched to your heart.

I see you
moving back
into the darkness
we have been,
that nameless woman
who leans from your skin,
who touches our lips
with silence.

Is she the dead
we know but never know?
Is she the past
still locked in our throats
like a stone?

Father,
I see you
bathed in moonlight,
our words
lost in the breath that is your body,
your face a moon's face, rising,

strained with light.

About the Author

Ron Talney was born in British Columbia but has lived most of his life in Oregon. He is an attorney retired from a private, non-profit legal aid program which provides free legal services to low-income clients. He has done political asylum representation for Salvadoran and Haitian refugees, as well as foreign election observation.

Photo by Michael Selker

He has published four books of poetry, *The Anxious Ground* from Press-22; *The Quietness that is our Name*, from Bohematash Press, as part of its Pacific House Series; *The Broken World*, from Stone City Press as part of the William Stafford Chapbook Series from the Northwest Writing Institute; and most recently, *Night Sky*, from Stone City Press.

His poems and essays have appeared in numerous journals, quarterlies, newspapers and anthologies, including *The Prescott Street Reader* and *Poets West*.

Ron Talney lives in Lake Oswego, Oregon with his wife, Linnette.

LaVergne, TN USA
16 September 2010
197282LV00004B/4/P